I kind of thought the **alpacas** were a metaphor until we got there

A catalogue record for this book is available from the National Library of New Zealand.

Soft cover ISBN 978-0-473-53053-2

Cover design by Amanda Sutcliffe

This book has been printed using sustainably managed stock.

Design & layout www.yourbooks.co.nz

Printed in New Zealand by www.yourbooks.co.nz

I kind of thought the alpacas were a metaphor until we got there

KIM FULTON

Contents

Play it again, Sam 6
Cassio and Desdemona 8
A box of Led Zeppelin cassettes 10
Physics Department, Avondale College 12
Social network 14
Grand Central, Hamilton 15
Dark Side of the Rainbow 16
Flat crawl 19
I sound my barbaric yawp over the roofs of the world ... 22
I kind of thought the alpacas were a metaphor until we got there 24
Shortcut through a churchyard 26
What we worried about in the nineties 27
If there were no flowers in the Garden of Eden 28
On the Road 30
Eden Park, Kingsland 31
Coastal Pacific Railway 32
Back to the Future Day, October 21, 2015 33
The last time I saw him 34
Where the cinema used to be 35
Park Road, Hamilton 36
Cape Foulwind, West Coast 38
The last crusade 39
Half-asleep on an airport bench, Kuala Lumpur 42

At a pub on the outskirts of Dublin 44
April in Paris 45
Curse of the colonel 46
A pirate once 48
Maungakiekie 50
This is it, Ruahine Range 52
The old Presbyterian church, Eketahuna 54
Grace Cathedral, San Francisco 56
Scotts Landing 57
When the planes hit the Twin Towers 58
A towering oak, a lingering summer 60
Fireworks on a field by the Manawatu River 62
Temp work, Bethells Beach 63
Salisbury Street 64
Raised Presbyterian 65
Carpark for rent 66
Koshien Stadium, Nishinomiya 68
Safeco Field, Seattle 70
Playing for keeps, Sausalito 72
A campus at night, Palmerston North 74
A newsroom after deadline, Westport 76
Farewell, My Lovely 78
Ko Maungakiekie te maunga 80
About the author 82
Acknowledgements 83

Play it again, Sam

is an immortal line
never actually spoken in the movie but
retroactively invented – a reminder of the
way we misremember,
the way we reinvent the past to
capture its essence – Ilsa's plea for Sam to turn
back time or the nights we spent
in the makeshift jazz bar in the garage
of our first flat.

I think of it most
as I see summer in and out,
him asleep on an overgrown lawn
and her playing Hupfeld on the piano
we'd wheeled in from two streets over.
The drug dealers next door
threw rocks at the corrugated iron roof and I
ate the first strawberries of the season
sitting on a second-hand sofa.

It was our local version
of the Casablanca gin joint created
in Burbank, California – a bar in a film
I watched over and over that year
on the off-chance Rick would choose
love over duty this time around.

Here six-packs of beer replaced brandy
and hand-painted portraits passed
as art. It seemed it was always summer
though I know that recollection to be as false

as the line never spoken at a bar
invented for a film I wish
I could play again in the flat with fairy lights
on the walls
and a piano in the garage,

but we were gone
too soon
to another house on the other side of town,
a family suburb, an upgrade,
a roof that didn't leak and a sensible spot
between the kitchen and the living room
for the piano.

Cassio and Desdemona

The scene is eight o'clock English in our final year of high school.
Cassio and I have come straight from cross country training
to read aloud the final act of Othello. I am Desdemona.
Yesterday Bianca handed Cassio the handkerchief
that would end my life and I recalled his terrible hay-fever
the afternoon we pulled the trucks from our skateboards
and used the decks to ride the craters
of the city's dormant volcanoes.

I feel sorry that it will be over soon, the play, this class,
a group thrown together each weekday morning
to live out multiple realities.
Earlier in the year we tracked the Ace of Diamonds Gang
in Owen Marshall's short fiction
and watched Anna Paquin earn her Oscar in The Piano.
Last month we prayed together for
our schoolmate who'd died on the football field outside.

Cassio puts on an impassioned performance
during his final fight scene
perhaps still coasting on the adrenaline of that morning's run.
Sitting side by side on desks in our school uniforms
I remember visiting him in hospital
after Roderigo put a hole through his lung at taekwondo.
I brought him a pot plant.

Our teacher lectured us on the many manifestations
of grief the morning the news spread
of the football captain struck down.
The team saw out the season in black arm bands,
then normality returned, cruel as it seems.
The field was blessed, a tribute match played,
a truck arrived to take away the flowers piled at the flagpole.

"That death's unnatural that kills for loving," I read,
then lose my place, distracted by the sound of shuffling
coming from a gym bag at the back of the room.
Emilia and Iago started dating last summer
and have shared custody of a rabbit.
Its handover occurs in eight o'clock English while
the rest of us work to keep our teacher oblivious to the fact.
"Soft you; a word or two before you go,"
Othello reads, as the ghost of Roderigo threads
a fennel stalk through a small opening by the zipper.

A box of Led Zeppelin cassettes

The mural of dogs playing poker on the brick wall
of the pool hall didn't bring to mind Coolidge,
who I'd never heard of at fourteen,
but Orwell, whose novel about an anthropomorphic
animal revolt was on that year's reading list.
Earlier in the day a stranger had stopped me
on the Margan Ave stretch of my paper round
to offer me a box of Led Zeppelin cassettes.
I like that detail because it places the poem

in suburban west Auckland at a time
when cassettes were no longer of value
to someone like him but were to me, fourteen
and lugging a backpack of papers around
my neighbourhood to pay the bills,
the bills being my share of the ten-dollar
charge for an hour of pool, another dollar or two
to programme Zeppelin into the juke box.

I had a snooker table at home and,
now, a box of Led Zeppelin cassettes
and so I didn't really have reason to work
for spare change to spend inhaling carcinogens
at local dives. Of course, if I'd stayed home
I never would have come across the cassettes
in the first place or had the opportunity to
ruminate on my half-grasped understanding
of Orwell's ideologies around work.
Our lives are miserable, laborious and short,
he said. It seemed an exaggerated notion to me
or at least outdated. The world had moved on
from his tales of oppression.

Coolidge's poker dogs were commissioned
to advertise cigars but became a symbol of working
class culture. They hung in the kitchens of
homes across America in 1978
as Robert Plant recorded "All of My Love" –
his tribute to a son dead at five while he was on tour.

I did not know the context behind it on those
slow afternoons inside smoky pool halls, his insistent
expression of fading love drowned out by the clatter
of the break and the voices of my friends.

Physics Department, Avondale College

Rumour was he didn't have a university degree
but rode a pushbike across the southern states in the sixties
which was qualification enough to teach the fundamentals
of quantum theory to twenty-five impressionable teens
staring out windows. Nobody knew why
he played the opening credits of Gilligan's Island
at the beginning of every class and nobody asked.

We calculated how fast the earth would have to
spin before it propelled us off and what the length
of a day would be. You didn't have to understand
the maths. It asked only a kind of faith
in the man who once worked a suicide hotline.
He said he told a caller who wanted to kill himself
to wash the dishes, which had something to do
with grounding him in the world.
It's good to help others, he concluded. It didn't
take a university education to understand that

physics was no more than the study of
matter and energy – that which occupies
space and its capacity to move. I thought
of his class as I passed the phone booths at
the foot of the Golden Gate Bridge, advertising
crisis counselling for those who had come this
far but hadn't made up their minds yet.
Before he stood at the head of a classroom
spouting stories and expounding equations
he was the voice at the end of a line, a sound
transmitted as signal and wave
and received over a great distance.

Social network

The owner of the wallet dropped in a downtown carpark
is a Samoan who loves Holdens and eating outdoors.
His friend count reveals he is no more or less gregarious
than me and I wonder what else we have in common.

This is how people fall in love these days,
not that I have any intention of falling in love
with the man in the photo on the pub table in front of me.

I wonder if the last person ever to write
their phone number on the back of a beer-soaked bar coaster
knew they were seeing out the epoch
where the speech Bogart delivered to Bergman
beside the plane at the end of Casablanca was possible.

And there would come a day when we could
no longer really lose a person while they were breathing,
when we'd know exactly where the one who got away
got away to and what they had for breakfast.

Hotcakes, it turns out, with maple syrup in an
antique-looking glass bottle that lends itself well
to Instagram's vintage filters. It's a scene manufactured like
something out of an old-fashioned film,
a man sitting outside a central city café, sporting half a smile,
not for the face behind the camera but some
far-off, unknown admirer.

Grand Central, Hamilton

It was where I learned to like whisky,
the drink of choice of the girl whose 'flatmate wanted' ad
I once stumbled across and answered.
Cocktails were two for one on a Wednesday night.
This is how friendships are born and drinks of choice are chosen.
What we love comes down to little more than chance.

Her father came to stay one week and we talked about
Kahlil Gibran in the kitchen with the wooden floors.
We planted asparagus we never ate, and harvested
potatoes we never planted. Such is the nature
of generation rent, we no longer reap what we sow
or choose what we love, like a white chocolate whisky cocktail

I didn't have to pay for in the bar named after a train station,
that changed the face of Manhattan,
shaped the city the passengers had just passed through,
or were about to, or perhaps lived in for the moment.

Dark Side of the Rainbow

On Easter, we drank Vodka Mudshakes
inside a fort, built of pillows
and sheets,
while we synched up *The Wizard of Oz*
with *The Dark Side of the Moon*. For this
he gave his only son.

It's important
to get the timing right.
Start the album
after the MGM lion roars,
he's your signal like
the cock that crowed
before Jesus died on the cross.

A rumour once
circulated about a munchkin
who hung himself on set.
If you watched carefully
you could see the shadow of his
body swinging
from a branch in the back of a shot,
it said.

Well,
we watched carefully,
and never saw a life end,
but the collusion of the Pink Floyd album
and the movie
should have seemed undeniable
but for the band's emphatic denials.

Call it
a coincidence,
another one of our attempts
to organise chaos.

Regardless
of intention, the pairing became known
as the Dark Side of the
Rainbow,
a paradox of sorts, after all
a rainbow is nothing
more than light
refracted, like that passing through
the prism
on the cover of the album,
also known as a symbol of God's
covenant with man,
if you buy into that sort of thing.

We have
no proof of it – the truce
between mortal
and deity after the flood, or of
the dead man swinging on the set,
only of this

perfect coalescence
in front of us.
We are on the brink, you and I,
drunk
in a pillow fort
in our early twenties, pairing
a childhood classic
with an album our
parents owned.
"Balanced on the biggest wave"
the words went while
Dorothy
staggered along the top of a fence.

Flat crawl

Your friend
sidled up behind me
beside a trolley fire
started by the editor of the student newspaper
and asked me
what I thought of you.

I said I wasn't interested.
You drank too much
and didn't read, spent nights detaching street signs
from their posts. You had a garage
full of them,
which I realise now was just a
symptom,
of your youth.

You're only young once,
you liked to say,
the trouble being we were young then,
you and I,
and I could not honestly imagine a
time when we would not be.
Instead forty-five and sober
on the weekends,
reading Faulkner
by the fireplace.

I finished what was left
of my vodka mixer
and threw
the bottle in the bushes,
unacceptable behaviour
in the real world
we would enter soon,
taking sensible office jobs,
cultivating sober relationships and
putting down mortgages.

Even then I knew
I was halfway there because I
felt terrible about the bottle
I had just discarded by the roadside,
which a minimum wage worker
would have to retrieve,
getting out of bed
early to go to a punishing job.

Perhaps
his oldest
was starting high school
and would need his own space
soon but the renovations to his
two-bedroom home cost more than
he made in a month.

The next time I saw your friend
we were on the other side of town and an hour had passed.
Remember when the fire engines
came, she said,
as if reminiscing about a shared experience years ago.
We sat alongside each other
in a swing seat on a rickety deck
as one day passed
into the next.

I sound my barbaric yawp over the roofs of the world

The night had come to him in the form of a poem
as he sat in a cell out the back of the local police station.
This born-again poet was our student teacher, a man
who had spent his youth drinking and fighting,
fighting and drinking.

We were more interested in the fighting and drinking
than the poetry, a small group of children
without any special abilities left to fend
for ourselves once a week on a Wednesday.

I should explain: once a week on a Wednesday
the children with special abilities went to special
classes pertaining to their specific abilities
while the less talented among us remained in an all
but abandoned classroom to entertain ourselves.
We were not bitter, being too young to sense
the injustice of our situation, nor were we poets,

being too young to sense the injustice of our situation.
Poetry after all is emotion recollected in tranquillity,
which takes me back to the student teacher
who once sat in a cell at the end of a hard night.
Older and wiser now, he had taken it upon
himself to teach poetry to a group of misfits,

asked us to bring our favourite cassettes along
to class and speak to the group about the lyrics.
I don't remember which tape I brought or whether
I completed the seemingly simple assignment at all only
that my friend, equally lacking in special abilities,
jumped at the chance to share his Smash Mouth album.

He DJs parties in Iceland now, sounds his
barbaric yawp over the roofs of the world
like the speaker from the Whitman poem revived when
Robin Williams played an English teacher in the film
once voted most likely to change your life.

Not that I would credit the student teacher with
changing my life or that of my friend,
I do not even remember the man's name.
He simply provided a momentary reprieve from boredom.
You see, so much of that year seemed to be about waiting

in unsupervised classrooms for the young and talented
to return so the school day could recommence. Waiting for
lunch or the three o'clock bell, to be a little older, not too old
mind you like the man at the head of the class
whose fighting days were behind him.

I kind of thought the alpacas were a metaphor until we got there

She tells me one of the weirdest things
I ever asked her to do was drive across
country to an alpaca show.

I kind of thought the alpacas were
a metaphor until we got there, she says.
I say what for. She says I don't know,
just definitely not alpacas.

It was mid-July,
our warm breath sat in the air
of the hay-lined arena. The hair styling
of a black and white alpaca got us talking
about Elvis.

He began as the face on the covers
in my best friend's dad's record collection,
whose song about a hound dog
we were forced to howl
on the hard wooden floors of
our primary school days.

I only grasped
the symbolism of it many years
later – the way time passes
and relationships fail.

The alpacas were just alpacas
at the time
and had nothing meaningful to say
about our youth or friendship,

as they posed for snapshots
capturing the absurdity of it all,
oblivious animals thrown
together briefly.

Shortcut through a churchyard

The shortcut from the skatepark where the
intercity buses arrived to the flat with the piano
in the garage wasn't worth the blood on my hands
from the barbed wire lining the fence we climbed
using a beer crate the last wayfarers left behind.

It seemed an apt metaphor for growing up, though,
scaling a churchyard fence and bleeding.
Out on the street a couple that hasn't been home
for the night kiss against the bumper of a ute.
Inside I imagined Sunday School children reading
the picture book about the Tower of Babel I once found
among stacks of used Bibles at an October church fair.

The images depicted a world of one language
coming together to build a tower to heaven and
being scattered by race in punishment for their efforts.
At the time, and still, it seemed a warning
against resourcefulness or ambition.

That's what I'm thinking about as I commit this
victimless crime on a Sunday morning, a depiction
of retribution among dozens of cast-away Bibles,
each representing a death or perhaps a loss of faith, a choosing
of a life of small trespasses over the gates of God.

What we worried about in the nineties

I prayed for the chicken first
because it seemed most urgent.
She'd had a good life but stopped eating.

Next came the planned pursuit of tomorrow's
lunch break. I'd been challenged to jump from
the highest platform of the adventure playground on the hill.

Lord grant me the grace to stick the landing
and live to hear how The Hobbit ends.

I loved that playground for its danger and its
violence, its splinters and protruding nails,
naked trolls with spiral breasts carved into wooden walls.

We only worry when there is immediate cause
when we are young, sea levels and chemical warfare being
inconsequential in the smaller scheme of things.

The chicken recovered, regained her appetite
and outlived Princess Diana and Kurt Cobain.
The playground was demolished,
rotting wood replaced with plastic,
naked trolls tattooed in memory.

If there were no flowers in the Garden of Eden

"Incredibly, there were no flowers in Eden – or, more likely, the
flowers were weeded out of Eden when Genesis was written down."
– Michael Pollan

I was a Christian the Good Friday morning we planted
the crocus bulbs in plots gone uncared for
as our flat passed through generations of undergrads
in black band tee-shirts and worn denim jeans.
Easter had a magic to it then – something to do with
the changing of the seasons, and the clocks, the planting
of bulbs in a town where winters were long
but hope saw us through, and liquor.
The bulbs needed a cooling period

anyway. Couldn't germinate without those
winter months' waiting. With the first bloom
of the first crocus, you knew it was almost over,
the cool sharp nights in bedrooms with papier-mâché walls.
We pinned old sheets up to keep the warmth
of the communal heater in the living room
where empty bottles lay alongside textbooks, open
to passages about St Augustine
and the evolution of the angiosperm.

We basked in the last of the autumn warmth,
sweating out the toxins of the previous
night. In a photograph you stand propped up
on a shovel with your unkempt hair
and your lingering tan. Perhaps the photo is the
only reason that weekend remains in my memory,
which has seen fit to discard so many others.
The bulbs survived – sprouted in spring.
The land had not been cared for in a long time
but the soil was fertile.

The first couple surely witnessed such evidence
of eternal life, for if there were no flowers
in the Garden of Eden, where did the fruit come from
that gave way to sin, our expulsion
from paradise, our toil and pain?

The sheets came down, and the first flowers
were plucked and arranged in a vodka bottle
on a coffee table made of old crates,
forever dyed a gunpowder bronze from the fireworks
we launched off it one November evening.

On the Road

The two of us ride this less travelled track,
me to the sound of Charlie Parker's sax
with Jack Kerouac in the back.

A stranger
in a blue sedan is
three seconds ahead of me.
I know it's no way to fall in love but
there's kinship
in a constant following distance
even if it is
maintained through my persistence. It's not creepy.

Just that I'm a little lonely.
Lost too if I'm honest and beat.
Not as in timing but defeat.
Beat as in the generation
that hit the road riding on the rhythms
of that Kerouac paperback.

Eden Park, Kingsland

I don't remember the last time I spoke to the boy
I sat alongside the night Chris Cairns retired.
The game was tied at the end of the second innings.
He'd choked at the crease then again in the bowl-off.
At 11pm we were still in tee-shirts as we walked
to the train station sipping cokes.
I couldn't tell you who won that night
the first leaves of autumn crackled beneath our feet.

The foliage would be green again
by the time the new playing season started,
regenerated through a chemical process I once learned
and have since forgotten. I wonder what happens to all
the things I have forgotten – the names of players
once chanted, heroes reduced to answers to trivia
questions printed on the undersides of beer caps.

Not that he drank – the boy who'd stay
onboard an extra stop to see me home then
backtrack through his troubled neighbourhood on
foot, shielded by his fighter's physique and faith.
We travelled fearless through those nights,
fading from memory like the knowledge of
the process that makes a hardened bud bloom.

Coastal Pacific Railway

The track winds past montbretia
and fishermen idling on rocks, and vineyards
where the sun and soil are harnessed.

Last night I sat on the deck of a pub with a
Swiss stranger cycling the length of the country
and told him about my newsroom job,
on the opposite coast, the old printing press in the
adjoining shed and the nights it failed, the courtroom
across the street where softened criminals sobbed on the stand.

It all sounded quite beautiful, he said.
I assumed something had been lost in translation.
It is clear to me now, how things are distorted
not by distance but by proximity.

The train presses on past council staff
spraying weeds on the roadside,
bait drying hard on a hook in the midday sun,
summer workers sweating for small
wages between rows of ripening fruit.

Back to the Future Day, October 21, 2015

The date came and went without
the help of a flux capacitor and I still don't
have a hoverboard. A battered but not beaten
Michael J Fox plays a lawyer with
questionable morals on a drama for CBS,
a profession abolished in the cult classic.

Meanwhile, I spend my weekends at a hobby I'm
ten years too old for – riding an off-road
skateboard across local pasture preparing for
the day Mattel works out how to defy gravity.

The Cubs almost made it to the World Series
as the film foretold, but fell short in autumn of
their promise in spring – a destiny laid out before
them disappearing like a fly ball lost to the sun,

setting now behind a long dormant volcano veiled
with grass on which sheep graze and I ride
more cautiously than I once did. I'm not scared
of an eruption but more minor and immediate threats,
a loose rock, a stray branch, unforeseen obstacles in my path.

The last time I saw him

He was half-naked
eating cold pizza out of the back of a van.
I think it's best to be honest with you from the beginning.
This is neither love poem nor elegy
in the traditional sense.

The "he" refers to an old friend
rather than a crush, "last" to most recent not final.
We're seeing Jumanji this weekend,
and could stay close for fifty years after that. Who really knows
for sure when the last time will be the final time.

The last time I saw him
his eyes were cast down to the
gravel of the parking lot alongside the
west coast beach where we had spent
the last day of the summer break.
By that I mean final,
tomorrow he would rise early and ride
his push-bike to work.

We hadn't realised how late
it was until high tide took us by surprise,
saltwater soaking the corners of towels,
laid out earlier on scorching sand.

Where the cinema used to be

All that dared to be part of a city's
lasting landscape lost itself like
riffs rising from an underground blues bar.

Do you remember the way this avenue looked
in late summer before the music shop moved
and the movies shut down?

Time taking
unheard melodies and films
we might have asked somebody to see.

To leave us like life in a bay
on an outgoing tide, yearning
for that place we lived which left us,

seaweed wilting in the sun,
pipis plucked from the sand.

Park Road, Hamilton

"Of all the streets that blur into the sunset,
There must be one (which, I am not sure)
That I by now have walked for the last time"
- Jorge Luis Borges

I said you didn't need to walk me the block and a half
to my house. It felt a bit old fashioned.
You told me to listen to the leaves rustling beneath
the streetlights in the early summer breeze.

You asked me who my favourite utilitarian philosopher
of the nineteenth century was. It wasn't a conversation
I wanted to have at midnight on a Friday.
You asked me about my favourite scene from Blackadder.

You drove me to every service station
in town the rainy night I had a craving
for Cherry Coke, then returned my forgotten
umbrella to my doorstep before sunrise.
It was what I expected of you.

There are things we will never understand
about each other – my tendency to wander,
why you've never tasted strawberries.

I think we really believed paths that cross once are bound
to do so again through common interest or chance
the day we said goodbye in your shared driveway
and pretended I'd be back and you'd be waiting
to show me the latest philosophy books in your collection,

while I'd made myself at home in your living room
logging onto your laptop with the date of your brother's
birth – your password for everything, then mine so
I remember it even now, six years after I saw him
for the last time,

and Blackadder would resume where we left off
the night we came home early from a party, as was our habit,
your brother just waking, as was his – Hugh Laurie young again
or still and strawberries in season, the elms in full foliage
on the street that joined our flats.

Cape Foulwind, West Coast

I'd think no one else had seen
the sun set from this secluded spot
but for the shards of glass
at my bare feet collecting its
December rays.

Tonight I'll settle
for the absent company
of unknown revellers and far-off
fishermen.

Don't get me wrong this isn't about
loneliness – the broken pieces people
leave behind – but summer days
stretching out like set nets
cast for sustenance, drawn in empty

as a stretch of coastline
accessed only by foot
over tough terrain.

The last crusade

I dream of coming across him in the bush.
Spotting him between a manuka shrub
and the thick mottled trunk of a kahikatea tree.
I follow him – keep to the track while he moves
in and out of sight just beyond it.

I don't think of him in waking hours
other than at times of change,
when summer moves into autumn as it did
that Easter evening in the bush,
or watching the NBA finals on television
while packing a bag for Montreal.

I wonder if he ever travelled or got a degree.
He wanted to be an archaeologist like Indiana Jones.
It's not unthinkable that I should talk to him again,
on a visit to his seaside town, run into him on some
forgotten piece of coast. Failing that, I can choose to believe
his history measured up to what his dreams were
and that's more than I can say for those who stayed.

It was a year when we lived our lives more collectively
than we ever had before, watched our breaths rising
together over lamps that marked the path from the campus
dining hall back to our halls of residence.
In late spring we selected our flat for our second year,
signed our first tenancy agreement and arranged all the furnishings
but he never joined us there, instead
returning home to the coast.

Our lives went on as usual but with one less person in them.
We used his dead uncle's washing machine until it broke down
then we took it to the tip. We had harmonica jam sessions at midnight,
spent evenings at jazz cafés or the blues bar we set up in the garage.

Back to the night in the bush our campus backed onto.
We had gone there looking for freshwater crays
after dinner. It was the night before the Easter break
when we would all return home for the first time.

I believe this is where the dream comes from
 – the one where I'm afraid to let him out of my sight.
I wake thinking of how different my life would be
if he was still in it.

I think of the childhood story he once told
of the summer day he almost drowned.
Pulled from a rip by a lifeguard, he sauntered
off down the beach without stopping to thank him.
After all, he had never asked to be saved.

Half-asleep on an airport bench, Kuala Lumpur

I think I'd like to come back here.
The promotional video on the aeroplane really sold the place.
It must be thirty degrees out and
I've always been a sucker for cities by night.

There is nothing to stop me from staying, of course.

I could drift off to sleep and miss my connecting flight
but then I might never see
the house where Marcel Proust composed
In Search of Lost Time.

I've heard a plaque is all that marks the site
of the cork-lined room where he sat a hundred years ago.

Not living exactly, but dying with more urgency than the rest of us.

It's not going anywhere.
The city waits patiently like
volumes of the novel lost in library stacks.

Restlessness is for the mortals
forever moving forward with eyes cast back.

He spent his final years
recording memories
in a room marked by a plaque
I once saw and
captured in a photograph
I keep in an
album on the shelf.

At a pub on the outskirts of Dublin

The owner of the inn across the road from this pub
buys me a Guinness with blackberry juice
to cut the bitterness he thinks I can't handle.
He says I can pay him back when he passes through my country.

He requests an Irish ballad the band doesn't know the words to
then appoints himself lead singer. Of all the cities where I've
never paid for a drink I think this is the most resilient.

I am befriended at the bar by an American who looks like
Kate Hudson and is as new to this city as I am. We're going to have
so much fun, she says. Maybe, I think, but not together.

It's nothing personal, just that I'm sceptical about her enthusiasm
for life in a country humbled by its history.
Best to stick with the innkeeper,
singing the wavering rendition of The Rising of the Moon

as rain falls softly on this Dublin roof and on the minus
three-degree street outside where a gypsy woman begs for
change, a new-born baby strapped to her chest.

April in Paris

I have always been sceptical of travel
writing, the way we claim closeness to places
that are not ours.

That's why this piece is about distance,
the woman photographing the man painting
the pianist playing on the walls of the Louvre.

I left the museum after an hour.
Snapped a photo of the Venus de Milo
and made my way to the bridge where
lovers hang locks
then throw away the keys
so they'll always
belong to this place.

It seems sentimental
but I thought of you and
how we'd never have Paris,
like a line cut from the first
draft of a love story.

It's funny how thoughts of things
that didn't happen
come out of the blue like that,
the story you once told me
about sitting on top of the Arc de Triomphe
with your brother watching the
near misses on the roundabout below.

Curse of the colonel

Superstition said the Hanshin Tigers wouldn't have
another series win until Colonel Sanders was retrieved
from the canal where fans threw him after
their team's 1985 victory.

The statue of the Kentucky Fried
Chicken founder was apparently the doppelganger of first
baseman Randy Bass and so was heaved into the canal
along with the real-life lookalikes of all the other players
on the winning team.

The urban legend gets a bit murky
after that. Fans seemed to believe it was the colonel's fault
their team was on an eighteen-year losing streak.

What is superstition after all but a miscomprehension
of the relationship between two things.

Surely we've all been there,
caught ourselves wondering where we would be right now
if not for the minor misdemeanours of our pasts,
in a high paid job in an office with views of the city or
at a bar beside a Mediterranean beach.

Certainly not sauntering from a train station
to a stadium to watch a losing team play, a single ticket
in my back pocket. Maybe this will be the Tigers' year,
I think to myself as I pass the fast food outlet
housing the remains of the statue construction workers
pulled from the river in pieces.

A pirate once

Looking back, he never explicitly claimed
his father was a pirate but the suggestions were there,
the eye patch, the story he told of the message
in a bottle he once found washed up on some foreign shore.

A cheeky kid, we assumed he had it coming
the morning the staunch Samoan from the year
above chased him around the playground
with violence in his eyes.

I wish I could remember more than the occasional instance
where our lives intersected, the day he convinced a group
of unruly boys to listen to my solution to the math problem
set out before us.

In court they agreed to call it a sickle,
but it was clearly a scythe, the weapon that killed him
the night he left a party in a suburb not far from
the one where we both grew up.

My newsroom eagerly awaited
the verdict on the alleged killer of the son
of a senior member of the Head Hunters gang.
He was dating a socialite, the daughter of the country's
once most respected broadcaster. She held him as he lay
dying. It was website traffic gold.

As we waited, I recalled the afternoon his father asked me for
the whereabouts of his youngest daughter. I pointed him
in the direction I had seen her walk ten minutes earlier with a friend
while I stood as a road warden just outside the school gates.
It never occurred to me to be afraid of the man with one eye.
He was a pirate once, but that was in the past.

Maungakiekie

We silently stalked the first spring lambs
and chased wild rabbits back into their burrows
the day Princess Diana died.

Later our parents watched the news coverage upstairs
while my brother and I played snooker in the basement

and I asked him how I was supposed to feel about all of this.

He said it was okay to feel sad,
and it was okay not to, we did not know her after all.

That was all I needed to know
to distinguish the experience in my mind from the morning we woke
to find a stray dog had torn into the chicken coop.

At Princess Diana's funeral
Elton John repurposed a song written for Marilyn Monroe,
whose death shook me more, long after the fact.

How do you find your way back in the dark,
were her last words on the silver screen before she took her own life.
I guess the drugs didn't work, the work was too demanding.

We are not taught how to process our emotions
I am told in a doctor's office twenty years on from
the day at the park. So, I set about learning,
fill her prescription and quit my job.

I do not mention the conversation with my brother that
contradicts her premise, wisdom offered as he
beat me at snooker at the beginning of the spring
of '97, when the nights were lightening
and I took defeat in my stride.

This is it, Ruahine Range

These winding roads always recall
Thriller, which was playing
as we drove them
the winter we were twenty-two.
Michael Jackson was just three weeks dead then.
Still, no more alive than he is today.
Snow settled on signs marking
our route.

I wasn't a big fan of MJ before he died.
I guess that's always the way
we mourn a loss that isn't ours,
we discover more than we remember.
His roots were in soul but
he'd become the biggest selling pop
artist in the world when he passed away
three weeks ahead of his comeback tour.

Tonight it's a Kanye cover
of a Ray Charles classic, an improvement
on the aging original in my pragmatic opinion.
You sit beside me again, your life
in my hands where you left it all those years ago.

You flinch as a car coming in the opposite direction
overcorrects on a turn, crosses the centreline,
regains control.

I remember why I left this place
as darkness falls and the temperature drops
well below zero. It was the same reason you stayed.

It was always too damn hot back home,
you said. You hope there will be
snow again tonight, but for me
the romance is only in the memory
of it, melting on the roadside.

The old Presbyterian church, Eketahuna

The skateboarders didn't reject the religious element
as much as the religious objected to the skateboarders,
when one of them converted the old Presbyterian church
turned ping pong club into a gallery of artwork
inspired by nineteen-eighties deck graphics.

The place carries reminders of its former incarnations,
pews between canvases, a hymn book still sitting by an
old wooden bat at what used to be the altar.

He planned to put up a halfpipe inside and attract
competitors from all over the world.

I was comfortable there, with a board in my boot, a dusty
Bible on my bookshelf back home. A skatepark always
felt more like a church to me than a church did anyway.
I should confess here I borrowed that sentiment

from the absurd Kinsella novel where a corn farmer
from Iowa travels across country with JD Salinger
gathering ghosts for his baseball team. A ballpark at night
is more like a church than a church, he says.

But I digress. The building housed the local Jazzercise club
for a time and I'll bet nobody complained, current
objections having more to do with the nonchalance of youth
than the misappropriation of a place intended for worship

of a different kind. Call it envy of their prowess in a sport
linked with rebellion since the days the pioneers took surfing to
the streets. It was not an abandonment of the old ways,
simply an adaptation to calm seas. Hymns no longer resonate

from the grand piano in the centre of the church, if you could
call it a church anymore. The lid of the instrument is a canvas
now, sporting the sort of artwork found on the bottoms
of our boards when we were young, worn away over
summers spent carving concrete slopes and grinding
metal rails, falling and rising with bloodied palms.

Grace Cathedral, San Francisco

Stained glass windows depict
human feats of science and philosophy
alongside stories of the scripture and
the legends of the saints
and let the light in just the same.

San Franciscans sit silently
remembering what faith felt like
before it was a choice
to be made, before the Scopes Trial
and the Stonewall Riots.

Perhaps I'm projecting,

and for them this is nothing
more than a temporary shelter
from the June wind,
a stopping point on a journey
to a bustling pier.

The coldest winter I ever spent was a summer in San Francisco,

is the quote I recall
seated in the light cast
by Einstein and Descartes
and the son of God, saviour of man,
as the fog rolls in over the bay.

Scotts Landing

It didn't seem dishonest or
underhanded at the time –
scouring the rocks under the
wharf for tackle after the
tide had receded and the
fishers had gone.

It was how I understood loss then.
Everything was retrievable with
enough care and attention.

Barbs of hooks glimmering,
sinkers and swivels buried by seaweed,
and one cool night near
the end of autumn a translucent and gold
lure that looked
like a piper swimming scared

over the
glistening shells
of mussels and pāua;
all that remains after the flesh has been swallowed.

When the planes hit the Twin Towers

It was my generation's John F Kennedy moment but
when the planes hit the Twin Towers I was sleeping.
Mr Moskowitz taught us maths in a room
with pi around the wall the next morning.
It was hard to understand that worth could be
conditional as I learned to solve for X.
Besides, my mind was on football as it usually was,
the ball I'd placed in the top left hand corner
of the net the previous week after riding my bike to the game
with the central defender from the opposing team.

After the match, we played Sonic the Hedgehog
in the living room of the unit with the shag pile carpet,
handing the controller over to her
middle brother when we reached the paths we couldn't pass
ourselves. The smell of dolma cooking drifted in
from the kitchen and her other brothers
played in the driveway with the cricket set
they'd received the past Eid.

Many years later the story emerged of a Muslim
woman removing her hijab on Sydney's public transport.
A siege was taking place at a nearby café,
hostages held a black flag with Arabic letters in the
window. We were all momentarily moved by an internet campaign
assuring Australian Muslims: I will ride with you.

We'd shortcut to her high school fields through a walkway
the new residential builds backed onto,
boots wrapped around our handlebars,
the early spring air hitting us with evening smells
of gardenia and queen of the night, of barbecues
and chicken shawarma cooking.

A towering oak, a lingering summer

She told me she once went back
and asked after herself at the
house where she grew up,
the property where we'd wake
early after sleepovers,
dew in the grass of the valley
where her dachshund sat
beneath oaks that didn't grow
from the acorns we found
on our way home from school,
but were there long before us.

Her grown-up brother
slept off a nightshift in the
neighbouring flat, the
mysterious man with the
fast car and the fiancée.

Summer stretched out until
Easter during those days
in her garden. The old trees
have been felled now and the acorns
we planted never took, I guess.
The valley is no longer
hidden from the street
or the street from the valley.

Last time I passed I could see
clear into the living room she
had returned to looking
for herself.

The dachshund was dead
by this stage, perhaps
buried in that valley.

Fireworks on a field by the Manawatu River

There are entire landscapes
I haven't seen by the light of day,
a cave where we slept beneath glow worms
at the end of a long tramp,
foreign cities approached from above
on quick airport stopovers,

a field where a match ignited a candle
held to the wick of a ten shot,
launched at a river I might describe as
hypothetical if not for my faith
in reason and the fact that

it took the life of a police officer
some years after I had left that city.
He had gone in after the family dog.
I interviewed witnesses from a desk
in a newspaper office up north,

scouring the street directory for the
names of the people who lived in
a neighbourhood that wasn't mine anymore
and was a long way from a candlelit field
I couldn't find my way back to
if I tried,

some memories
existing as darknesses
punctuated by quick bursts of light.

Temp work, Bethells Beach

That summer we spent chasing spinifex
through sand dunes in steel-capped boots
wondering why we'd want to spend
working hours anywhere else
was ten years ago.

I thought I'd be forever bound
to the group of misfits drawn together
by vacancies at a local temping agency
after I'd moved on, to jobs with steady wages
in air-conditioned office buildings,

the former convict with twins on the way,
the teacher in training
who helped him find God,
the recent widower whose garden
we all drank in come Friday.

As it turned out we left the past where it belonged
just like we always do,
the sand we emptied from our boots
before we left the beach,
the spinifex that eluded us
bouncing over windswept grass
and shifting dunes.

Salisbury Street

As far as I know
the kitchen roof still leaks
and a cobbled path still leads to a locked shed with a lost key,
the imagined legacy of past tenants inside.

I sometimes worry that given enough
time one can love and forget.

That house on that dead-end street
people entered without knocking
and left without saying goodbye.

As far as I know the paint still peels on the back deck
where you shook my hand then asked my name,
or it was the other way around.

Raised Presbyterian

you tell them when they ask, choosing your words
carefully and feeling instantly guilty.
You tell them the straight and narrow
didn't lead where you were going
but hand drawn maps under the passenger seat of
your Nissan Sunny could take them places
they've never known – a farm at the end of a gravel road
in between two forgotten towns. A house that smells of the thyme
and cheese scones the mother of somebody you
ought to have kept in touch with is baking.
You like to think you could dig that map out and go there one day
and if you did she'd invite you in but that's a different kind of faith.
You tell them it's a bit like the first
frost under autumn's blue skies
or falling out of love
but you know you've lost them.

Carpark for rent

It involves a property manager
and a bond, which raises the question
of the sort of damage you can do
to what is, in essence, emptiness,

a small piece of the world
somebody pays a fee to do nothing with,
then rents to somebody else at a higher price,
through a third party who takes a cut
for ensuring the right person
continues to do nothing with it.

I wish I could say it was the most
I ever spent on nothing,
but then there's the insurance I've paid
on houses that never got burgled,
cars that never got stolen
and a body that hasn't yet failed.

The neighbourhood's not even great.
Junkies barbecue outside a brothel next door
and every weekday a different pair of
underpants lies abandoned
in the otherwise empty street.

I like to think about the bonds
that never got returned,
tenants who revolted against the emptiness,
painted murals or erected
raised rose gardens.
In reality, I'm sure the realtors just took what it cost
to remove the oil stains
reflecting artificial light as rainbows.

Koshien Stadium, Nishinomiya

Tonight the Tigers play
the Hiroshima team with Cincinnati logos
on their caps
in the last game of a season
that started
when the cherry blossoms
were in full bloom.

I saw them
from the top of Mount Yoshino,
after a hard day's walk
preceded by a train trip from a rundown hotel
in a town you've never heard of,
sat on the peak
and thought about the way
fleeting beauty
is lost most fully when it was lent. I was
only passing through
this place, resting temporarily
on a mountain top
in a foreign archipelago.

Thousands of baseball fans breathe
air into balloons
at the bottom of the seventh innings,
release them
to deflate in a momentary spectacle.
They hang in the breeze
then fall like petals
on the field below, and on
the girls selling beer out of kegs on their backs,
and the mascot bearing an uncanny
resemblance to that of the
Philadelphia Phillies.

This is
a borrowed love,
taken and displaced like air
inside a balloon,
savoured and given up
in a collective
exhalation.

Safeco Field, Seattle

At the end of the third innings
a child races a man in a moose outfit to first base
for a discount on chilli fries.

I'm not sure what chilli fries are,
but still I'm rooting for the child
over the moose, like I root for the home team
even though this is not my home.

Safer to side with the masses,
I say. Call it risk aversion – that human tendency
underlying the business plan of the insurance company
this field is named for.

In the event of my death
my travel insurance will pay for the
return of my remains to my home town,
according to the darker part of the
policy wording that we tend to
skip over for the most part.

Suffice to know they
will shell out for lost baggage
or a missed connection.

White Sox strike out with bases loaded.
From my spot in the shade
I watch the Mariners make
their way back to the dugouts.
Somewhere in there this was dubbed
America's pastime.

Playing for keeps, Sausalito

I am taken back by the names of our marbles
as much as the
glistening colours, the connotations
the names carried then: *Sunbursts* like the
yachts my older brother perfectly manoeuvred across
the Manukau Harbour and *Cat's Eyes* like the
marine snails I pulled from rocks
as I watched him.

It was unthinkable then
that language
should mean anything other than what it
meant to me, an *Oily* recalling a slick on a rainy
night-time street seen
out the back window
of our dad's old van, his headlights casting
rainbows on the darkness.

Some names have held across seas
and years for me
to rediscover on the shelves of this quiet store
in Sausalito – *Turtles* and *Bumblebees*
three dollars a bag.
Others I have left behind,
the *Katipō*
named for our native spider,
the *Upside Down Crystal Cat's Eye*
I can find no record of
ever having existed outside my school gates.

A campus at night, Palmerston North

We weren't the first to fall in love with Yeats
or drink vodka straight from the bottle here
but perhaps it never occurred to anybody else
to risk a trespass charge to play Chopin,

whose notes rose from the piano in the basement
of the humanities building through empty midnight floors
while outside spring was just beginning
in the same way it always did,
cherry trees blossoming with
the bikes intoxicated boys in rugby jerseys
lodged into their branches.

"We sometimes go there at night,"
a new acquaintance had whispered to me
during an eight o'clock lecture on cell biology.
"The two of us have classical backgrounds,
she plays mean jazz piano."

I tried to imagine them
diligently practicing as children,
thought of the lives we lived before this
moment and would live after

campus security ramped up
and the rugby boys scattered
to office jobs in surrounding cities,
while bikes rested among
fresh foliage, a late summer
breeze catching the wheels,
turning spokes on an axle
this way, then that.

A newsroom after deadline, Westport

The rolling door's drawn down on the printworks
where paperboys and girls line up on slow summer afternoons,
their teenage conversations entering open office windows.

Isn't that what you got into this industry for anyway,
snippets of the lives of others drifting into your days?

Besides, their lives are more interesting than those of the
athletes and artists and bureaucrats you've interviewed,
whose names you'll drop in bars ten years from now,
the big stars who once graced a small town fleetingly.

Noah likes Kelly and Kelly likes Noah back
they report while the receptionist punches holes in
that day's edition and carries it to the archives out back.

I'd spent hours there scouring the files for the identity
of an eroding aircraft spotted in bush thirty kilometres north of
here.

Perhaps that was the cause of my demise in the industry
– always being more drawn to the old than the new.

The plane almost certainly wasn't the Brougham lost without
a trace attempting to make the first successful crossing of the
Tasman but might have been, according to my investigations.

The bush was dense but many had stumbled upon the
remains over the years, from the local businessman
whose sons grew pot there in the nineties to the elderly tramper
who said it was like something out of the comic books

that sustained him in this town when he was no older than
the kids generating distractions outside my window.

I think they'll stay with me – the paperboys and girls,
waiting for work to give way to more pressing tasks,
an image lingering on the periphery of memory,
a single engine plane rusting in a valley.

Farewell, My Lovely

Athens

It was thirty-two degrees, warm for May.
You were on the late bus to Syntagma Square.
I waited in a moonlit hotel room.

Double doors opened to a balcony
with a view of the Acropolis
where that afternoon I'd seen a tortoise
evade the feet of thousands of
tourists, all looking up.

Call it indifference or defiance.
We all have our reasons
for choosing the places
we do to spend our days.

They say a spur-thighed tortoise
can live a hundred years
in its natural habitat.
I don't know if this is it:
ruins two thousand years old,
a stray dog asleep under an olive tree.

Maybe it's not a question of place but of pace.

Midnight conversations rose from a courtyard
below while Farewell, My Lovely played in Greek
on a television set with rabbit-ear antennae.

In our early years
we shared a room in a house
half a world from here, where
the hallway light stayed on to quell
my night-time fears and
kept you awake.

Now we move
across a foreign continent
together and apart as interests dictate
(you care no more about the café
where Hemingway ate lunch than I do
the pathology of the spleen).

In a week, I will take
five flights back to the
rural town where I live and you will
continue on to Crete and Thessaloniki.

Until then we will sit together
at an outdoor restaurant overlooking the agora,
grounds for gathering lacking their former lustre
but more alluring for their resilience.

Critics would say it strayed from
the original tale at times but
retained its essence, the nostalgic film
following the convoluted but familiar
story about a life on the run.

Ko Maungakiekie te maunga

The steps where I sit are the location
of an old family photo of
all of us on a summer's afternoon, everyone who mattered then.
That circle hasn't changed a lot.
A handful of people have been added.
Others have passed away but persist in the memories places keep,
like the rules to a childhood game
after those who played it have gone.
That's on my mind because children's voices draw near.
They've given these steps the title of home,
which means different things in their language and mine
but in both represents something to gravitate towards,
something to run from.

The Māori way of introduction
allows us to identify ourselves by our landscapes.
Ko Maungakiekie te maunga,
Maungakiekie is my mountain,
but it is the first of many spanning
regions and decades, like the central North Island
giants we slept beneath during summers
of our teenage years, or the peak with a view
of the Nara prefecture
at the height of the cherry blossom season.

These steps and terraces were erected in 1954
from a bequest by Sir John Logan Campbell,
according to a plaque at my back.
As a young man Doctor Campbell arrived from Scotland in 1839.
In the founding of Auckland, he gave this park to the people
of New Zealand for their enjoyment and benefit.
He died in his ninety-sixth year, and now rests on the summit
of Maungakiekie, known as One Tree Hill,
which he loved dearly.

I can't help but admire
his resolution to rest eternally on the summit of a mountain
in a park shaped by lava flows on a volcanic field tipped
to erupt again in the next thousand years -
someone drawn to movement and stillness in equal parts,
a place's push as much as its pull.

About the author

Kim's writing has appeared in literary journals throughout New Zealand and overseas. This is her first book of poems. Her master's thesis explored indirect approaches to loss in elegiac poetry. She loves sport, particularly soccer and cricket. Kim previously worked as a journalist and is now a communications specialist in the tertiary education sector. She lives in Auckland, New Zealand.

Author Photo: Anuvindh Sankaravilasam

Acknowledgements

My thanks to the editors of the publications in which poems from this collection first appeared: Landfall 235, Mimicry 4, Poetry New Zealand Yearbook 2019, Scattered Feathers, The Unnecessary Invention of Punctuation, Geometry | The Open Book, Hue & Cry 8, The Pangolin Review, Ngā Kupu Waikato: An anthology of Waikato poetry, and Stasis Journal. Many thanks also to the lecturers who guided me during my time at Massey University, especially Bryan Walpert and Thom Conroy. Thanks to Glenn Colquhoun, who has been sharing his wisdom about poetry and life since our paths crossed in the Manawatu more than ten years ago. Thanks to Jen Stevens and Keira Stephenson for their feedback on drafts of this manuscript and Laurice Gilbert for her expert advice. Finally, thanks to my family, especially Jenny, Garry, Tanya, Dean, Jochem, Flor, and Jean, for their constant support.